COLORING BOOK

this book belongs to

_____

_____

_____

_____

VICTORIA

VICTORIA

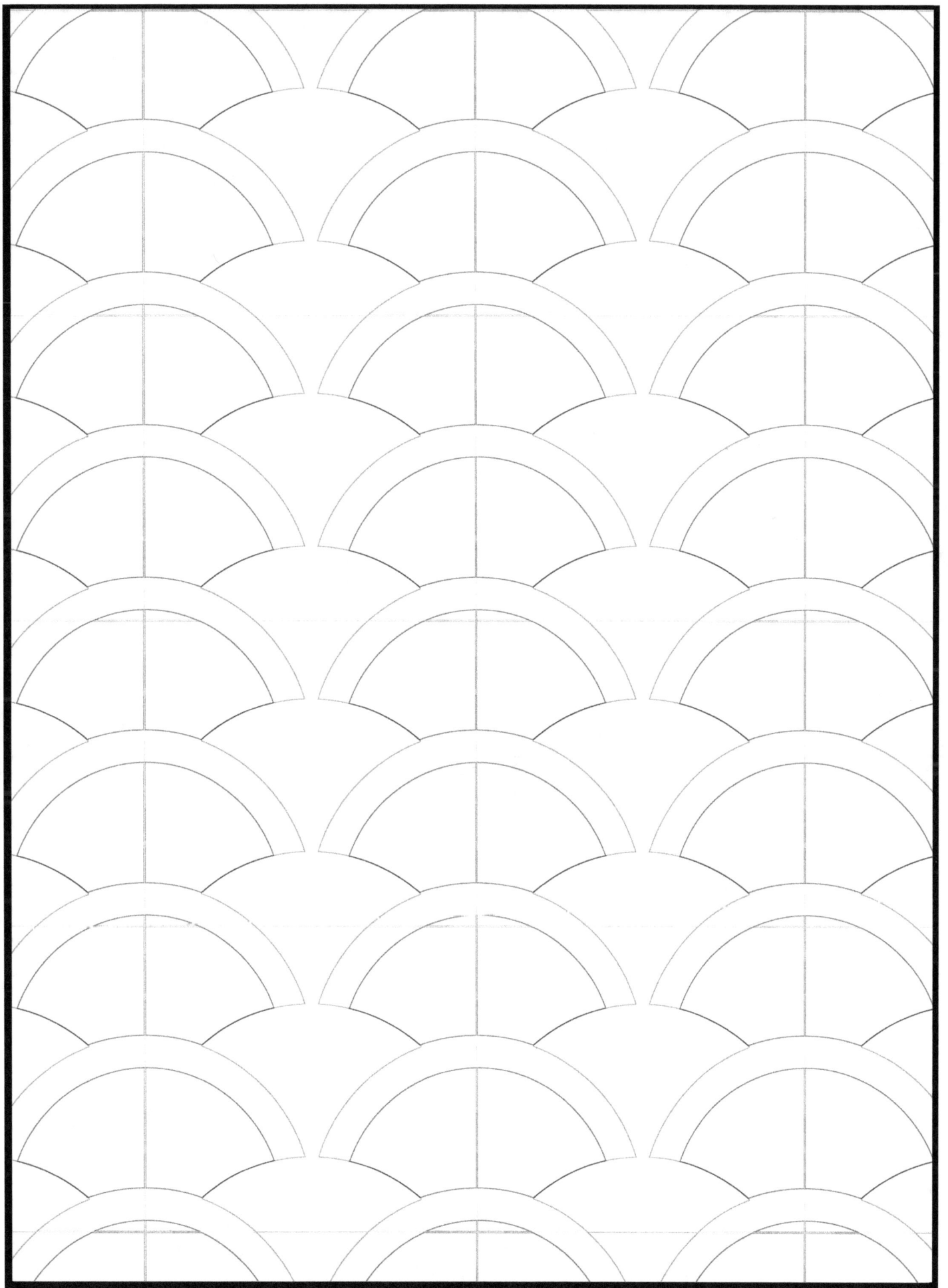

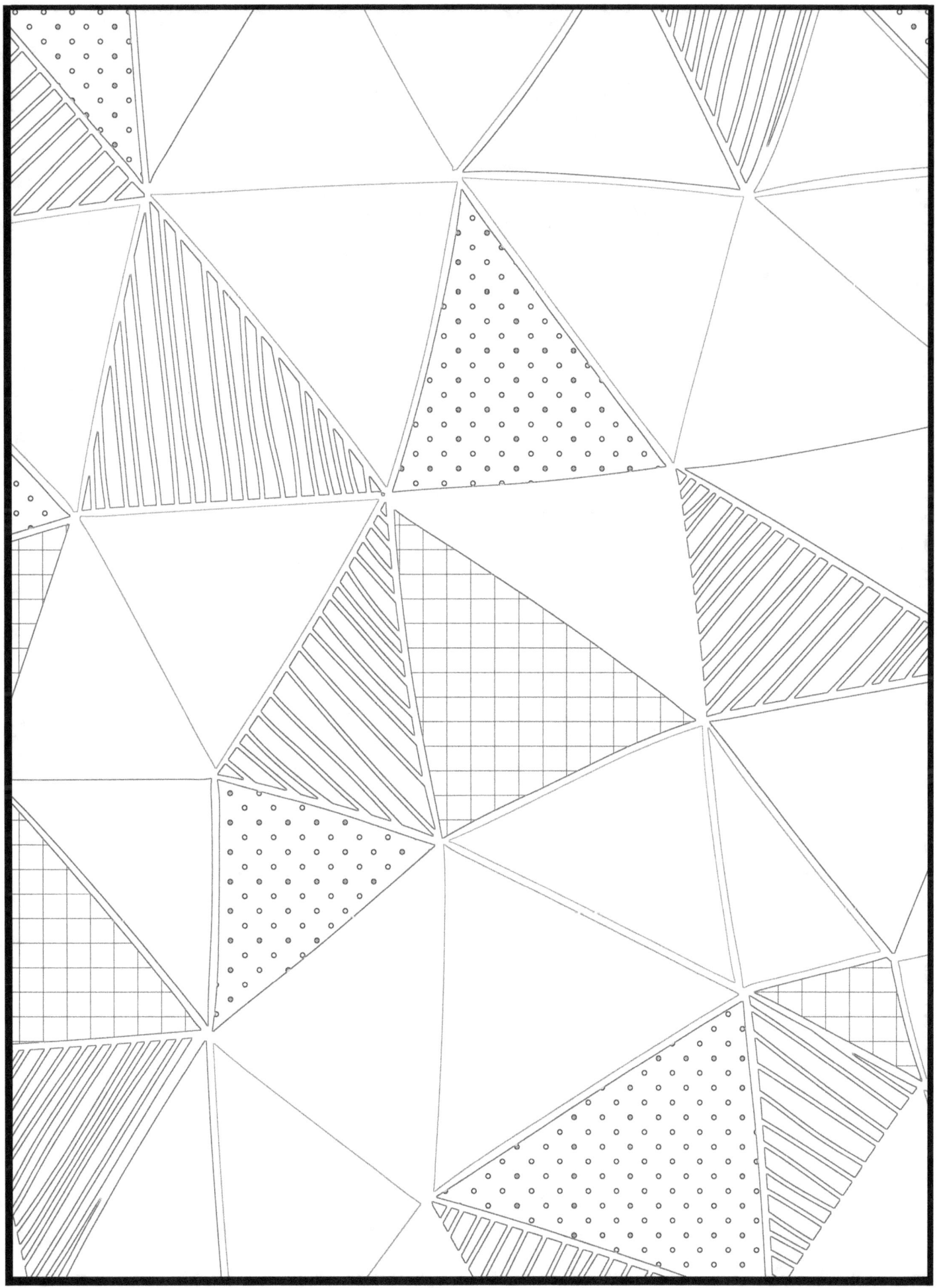

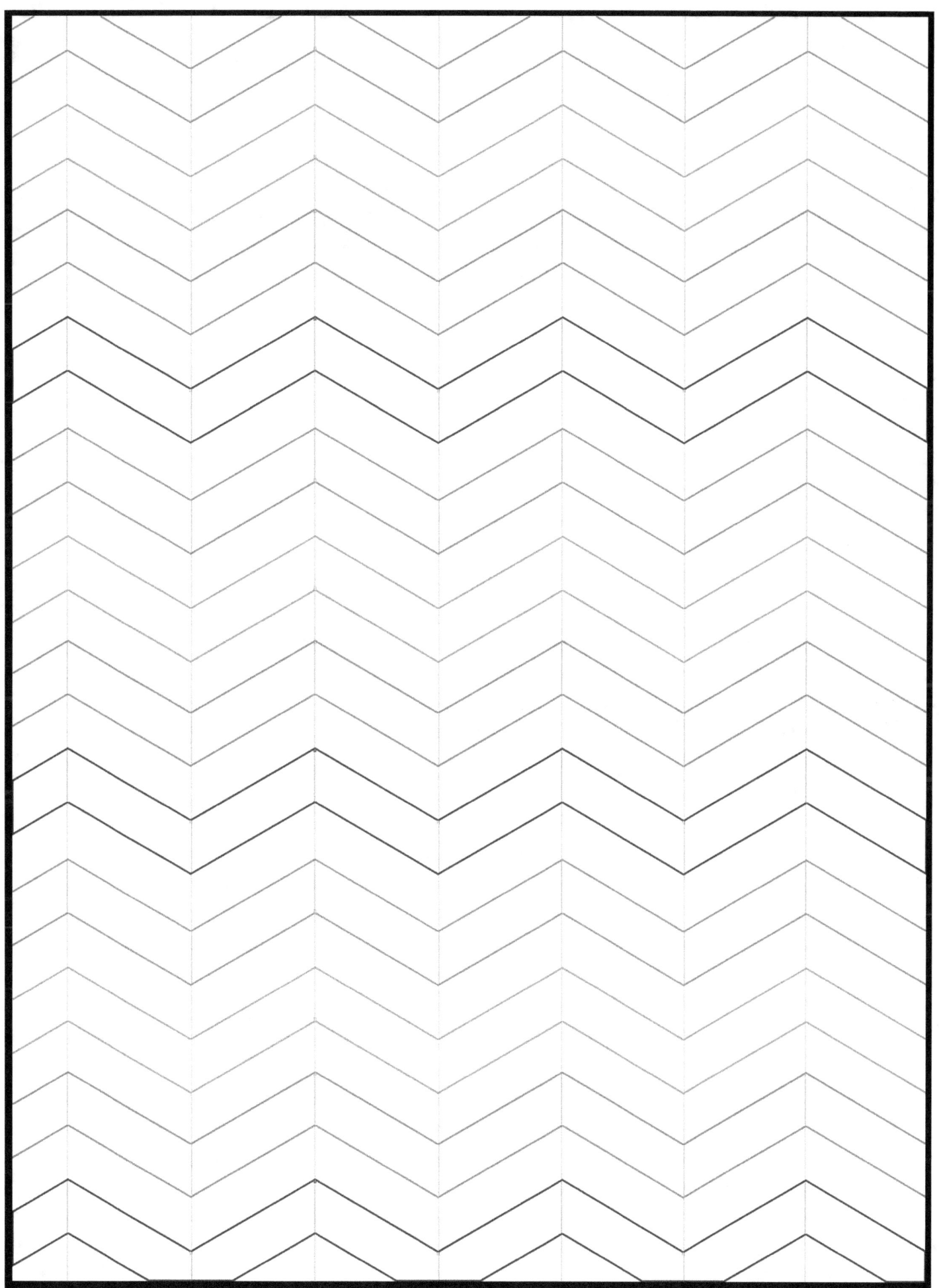

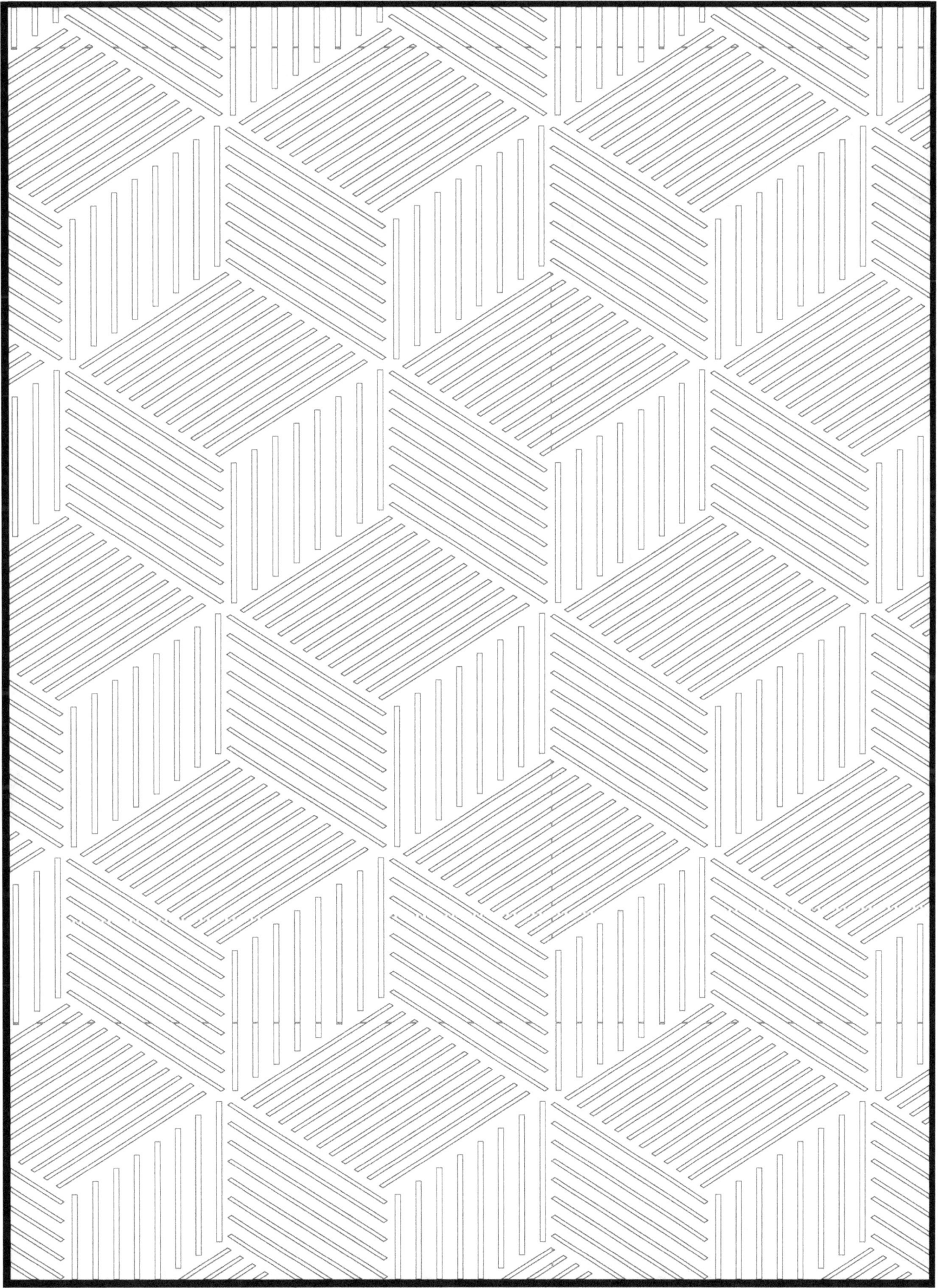

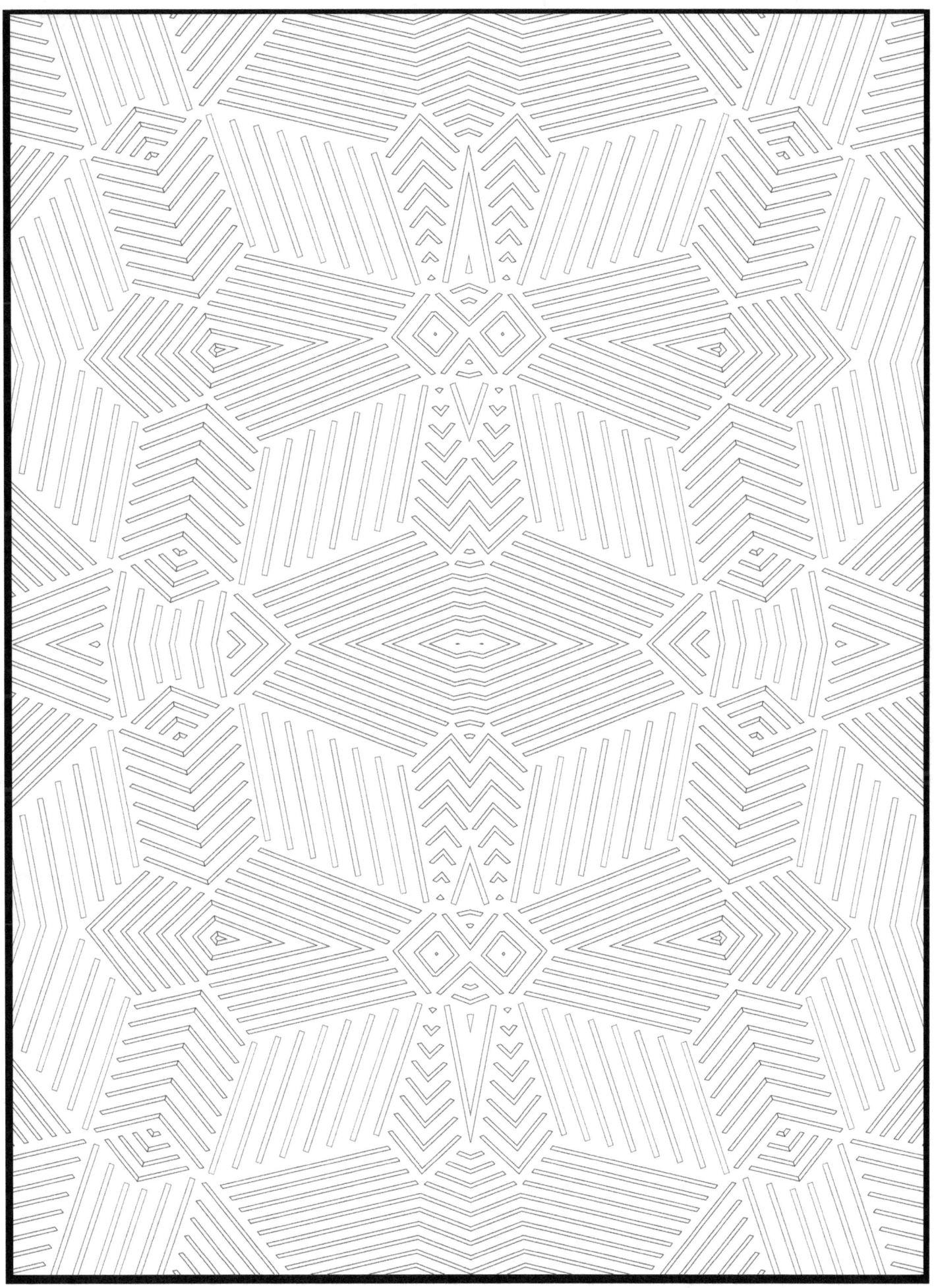

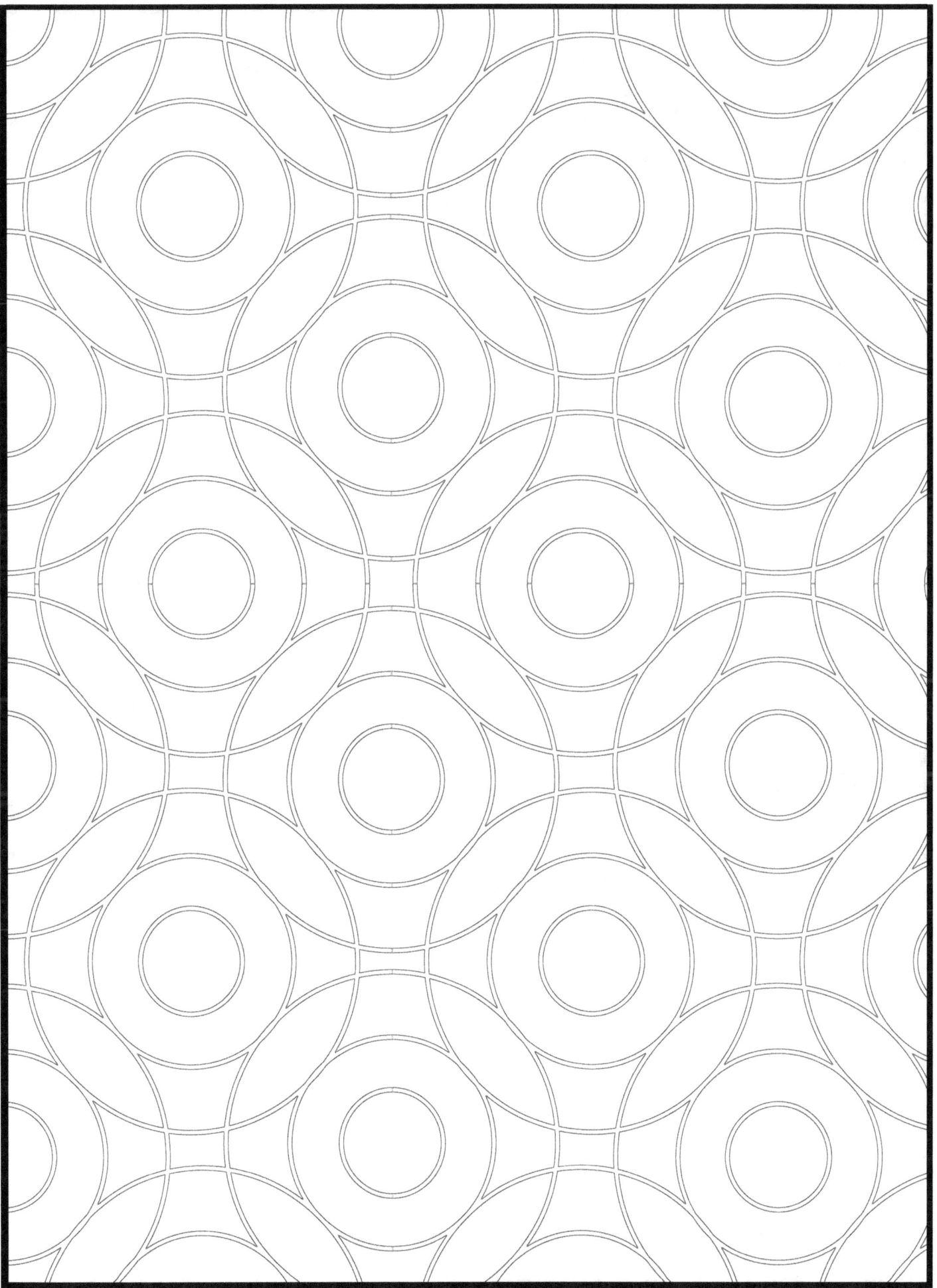

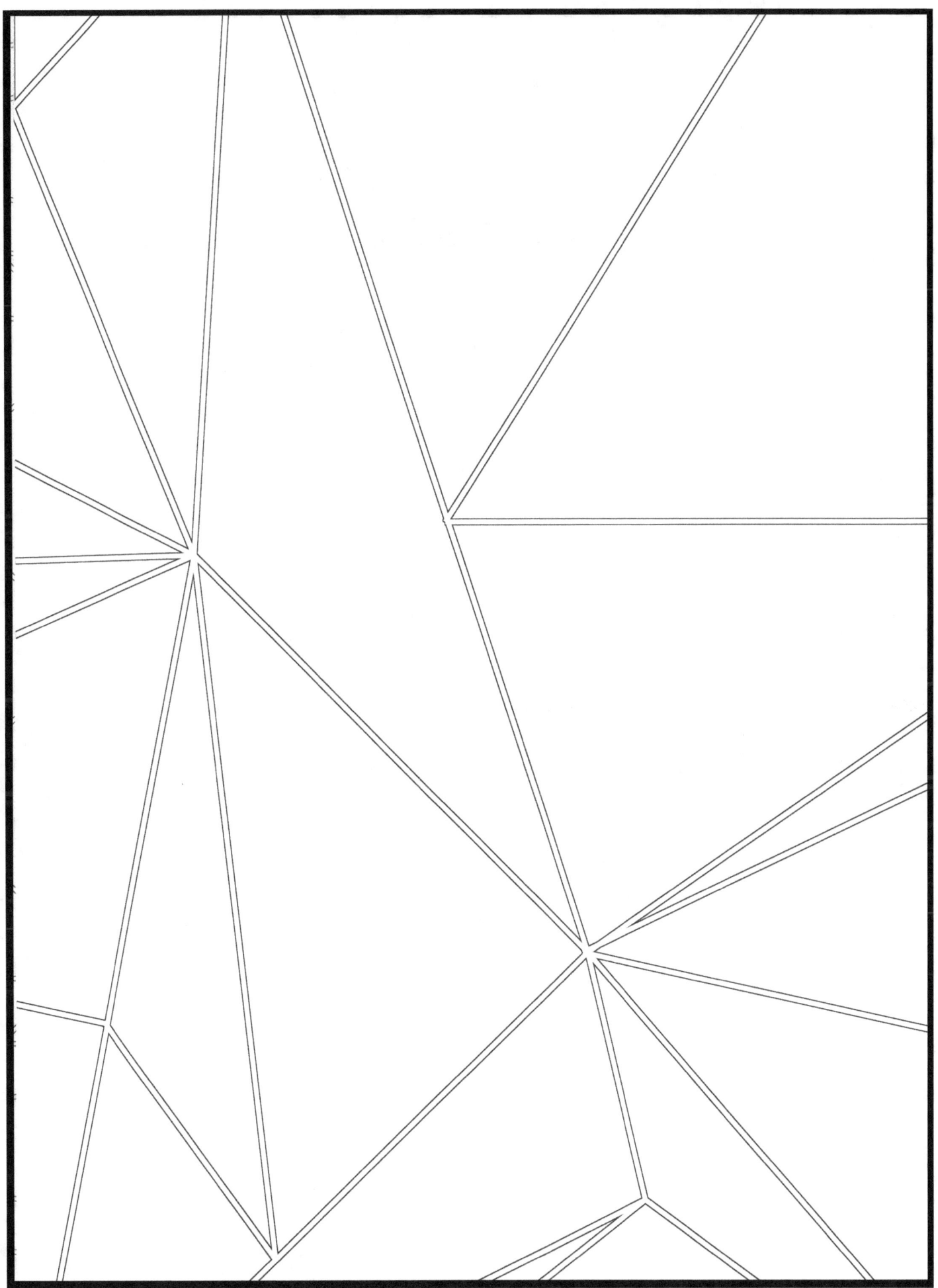

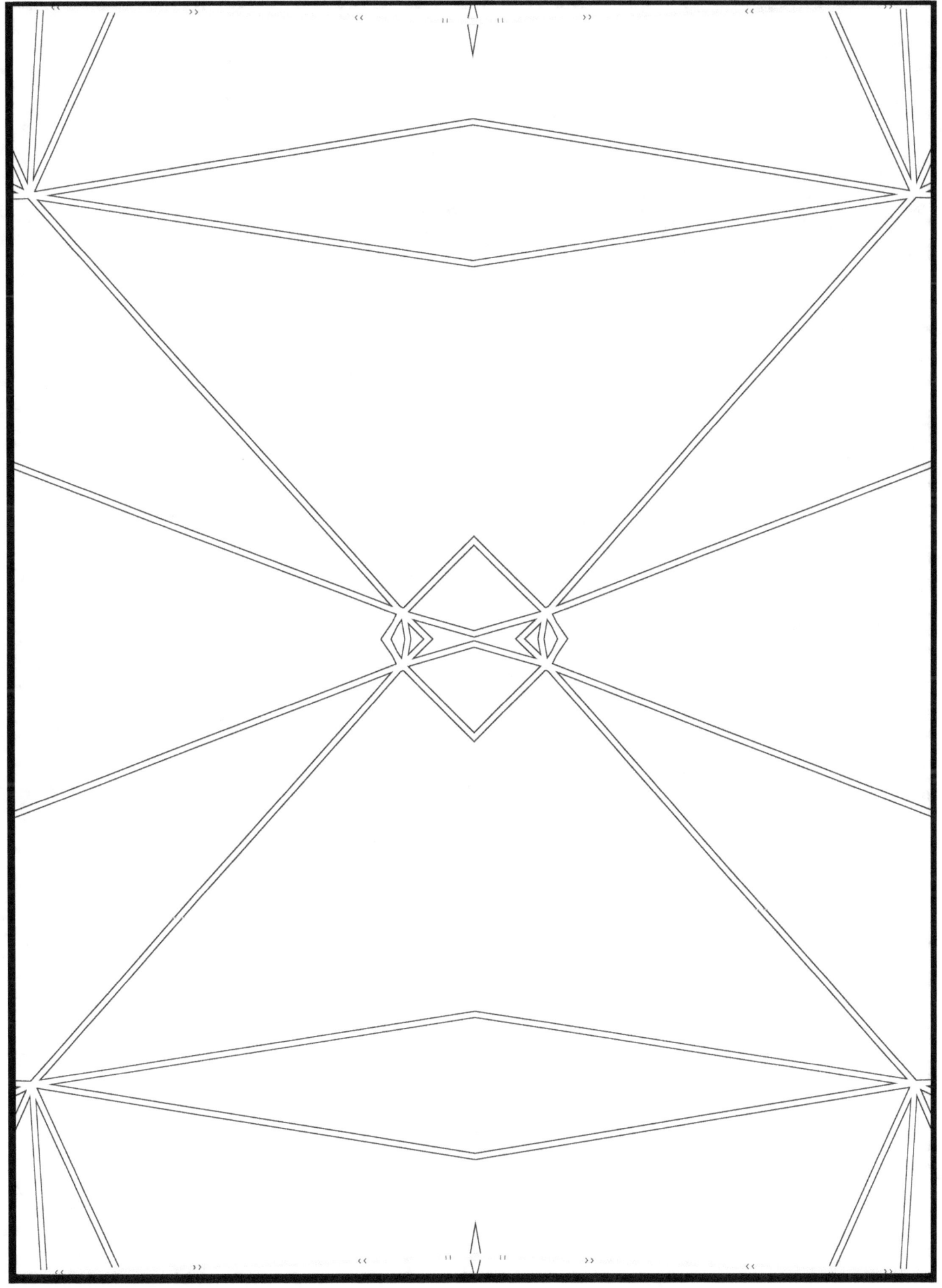

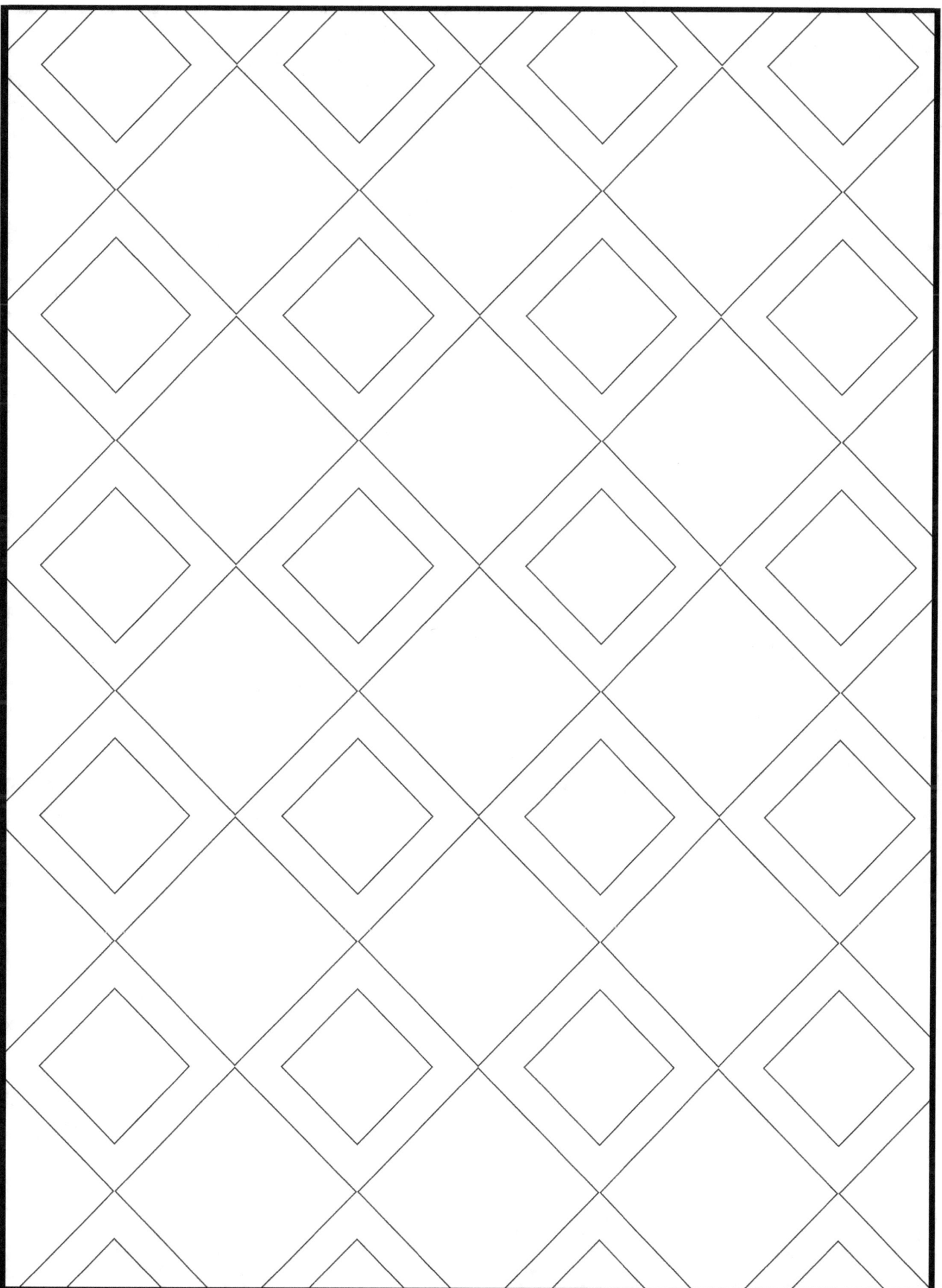

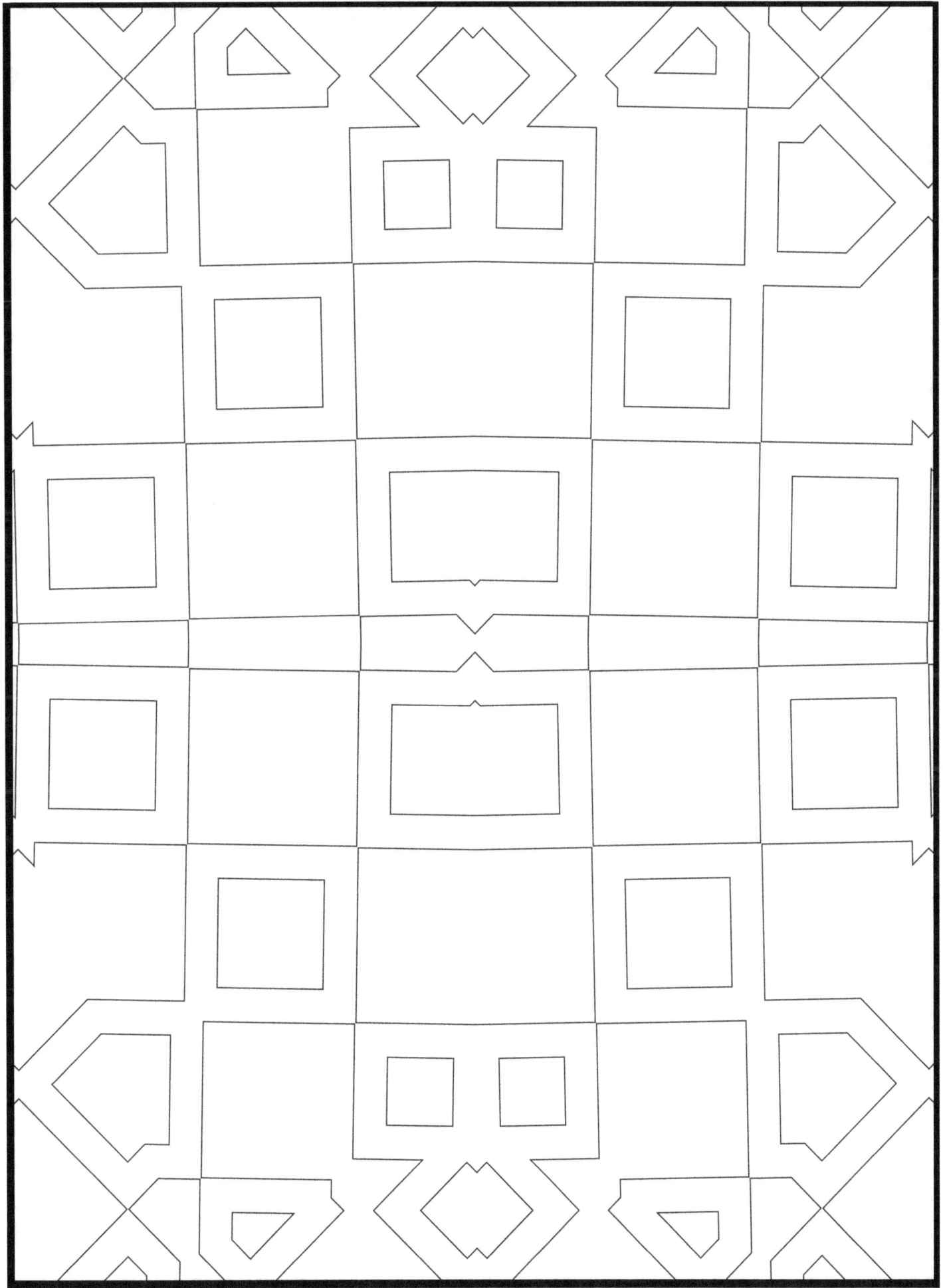

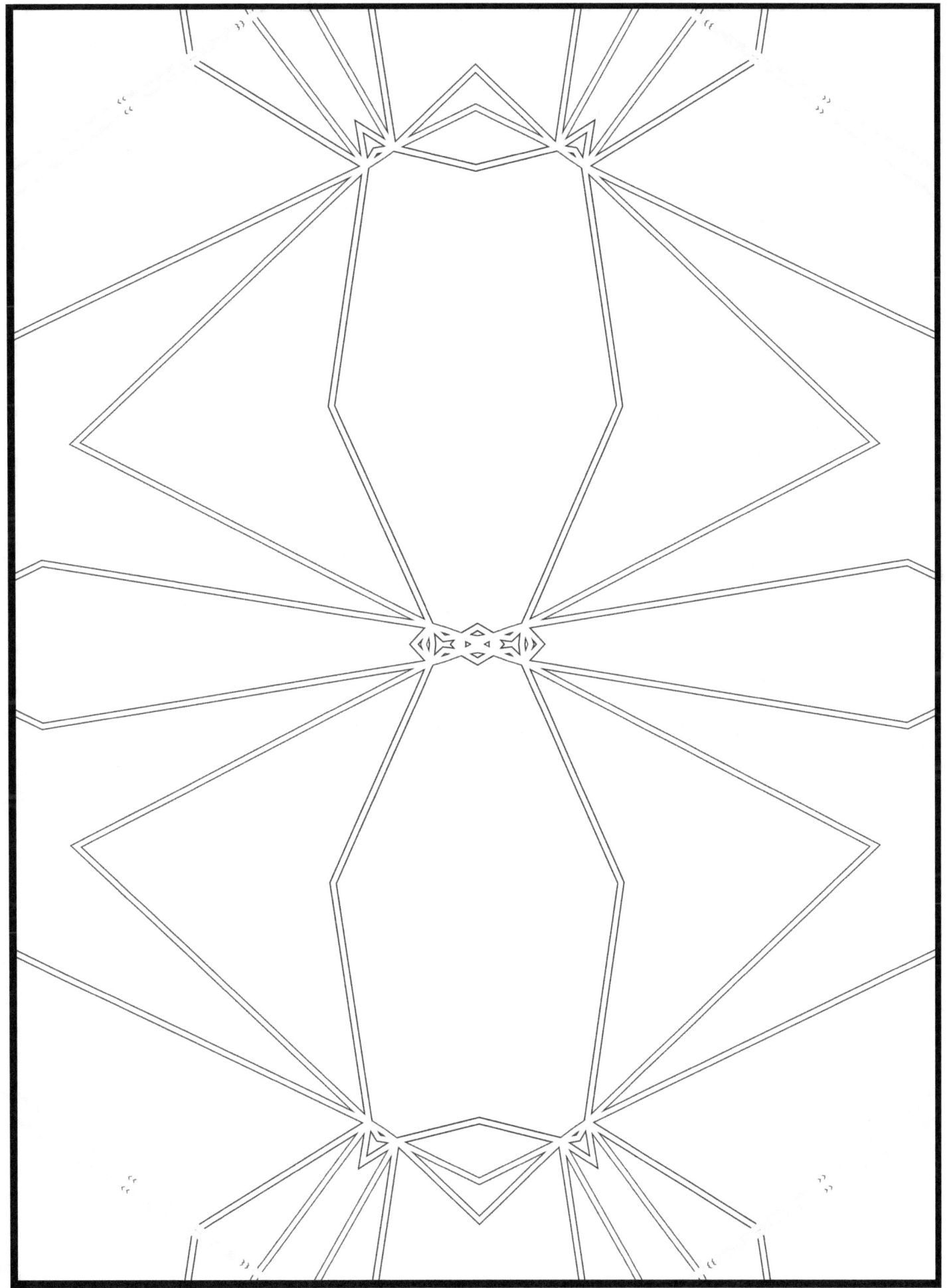

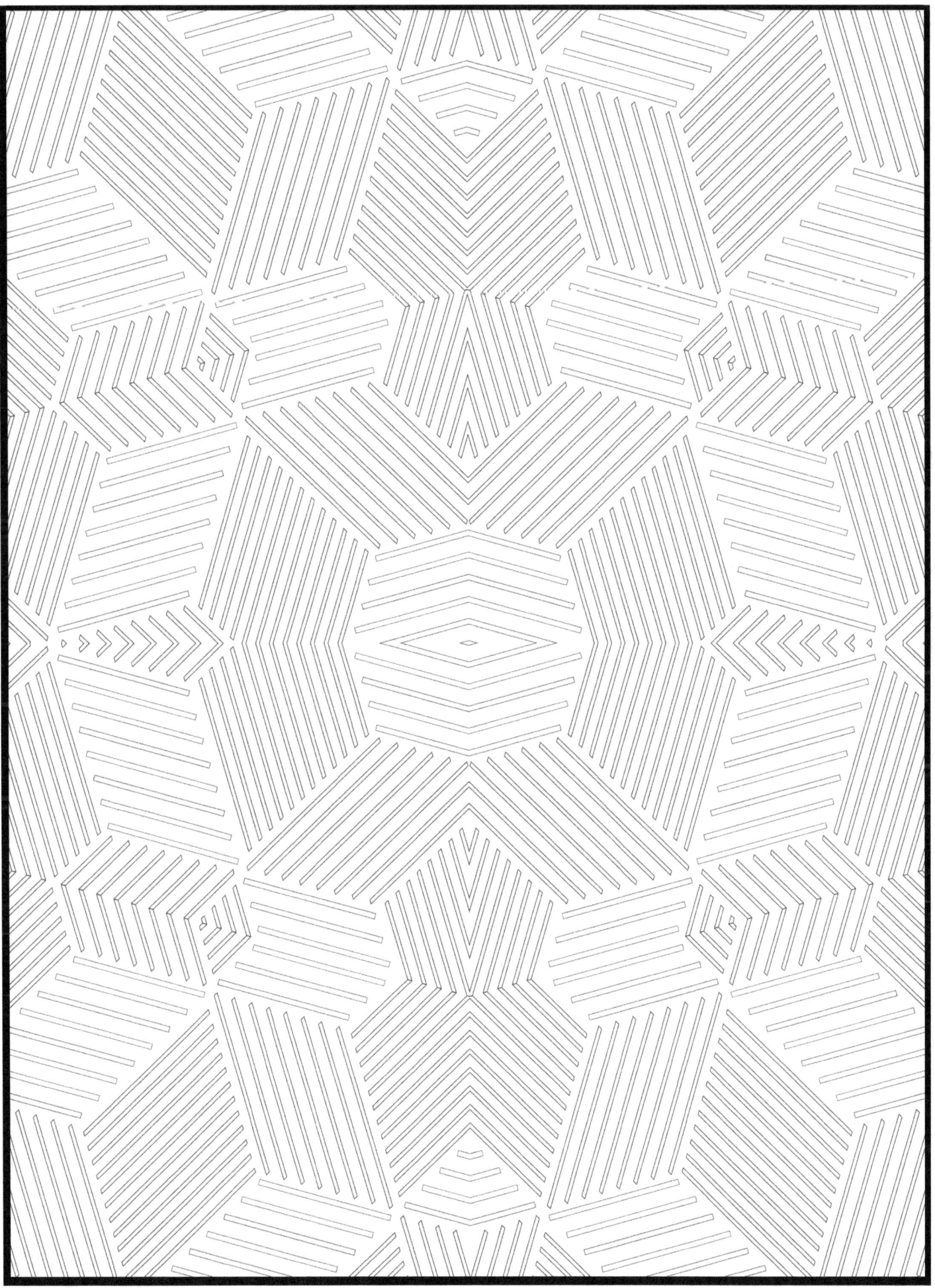

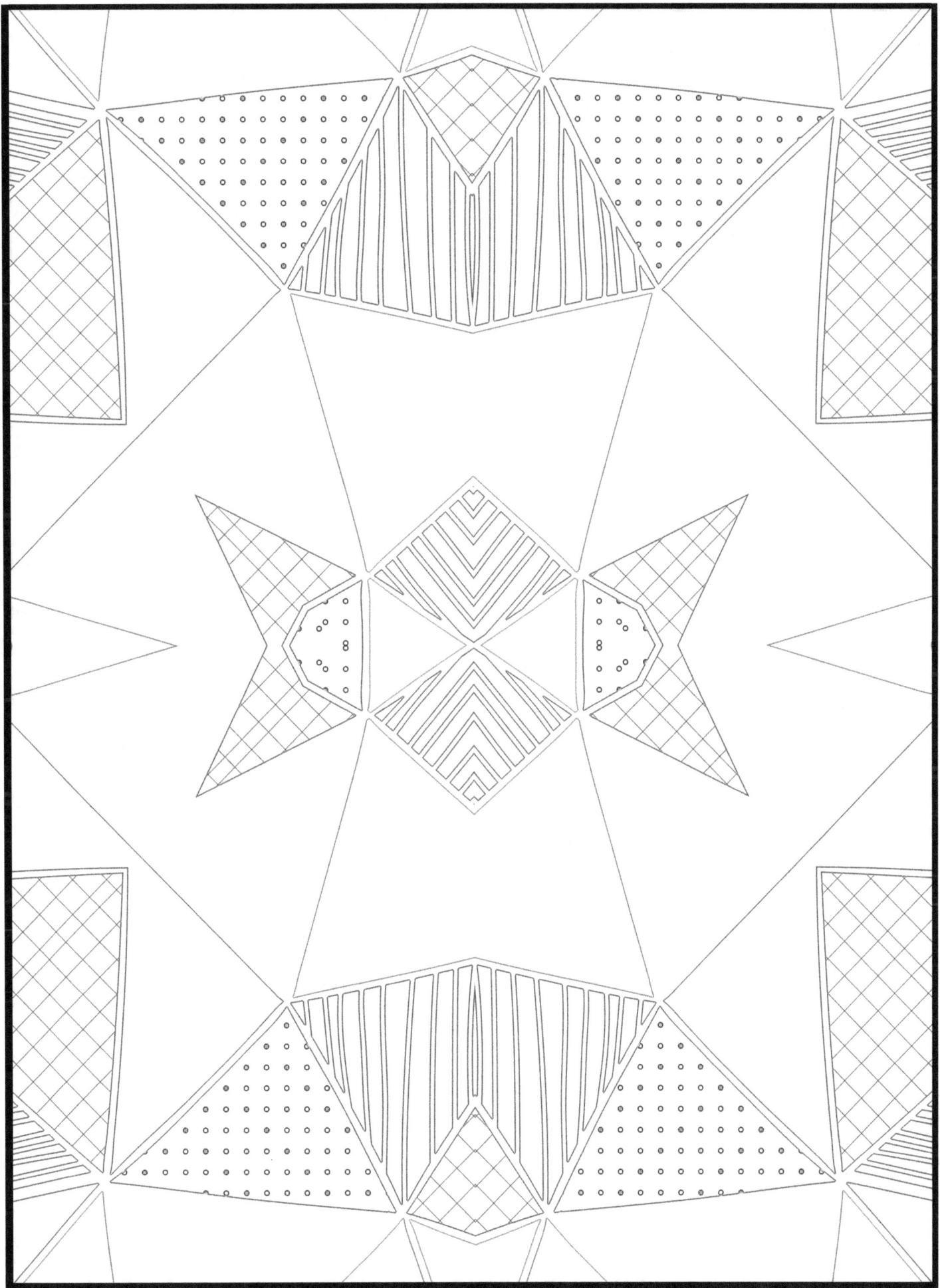

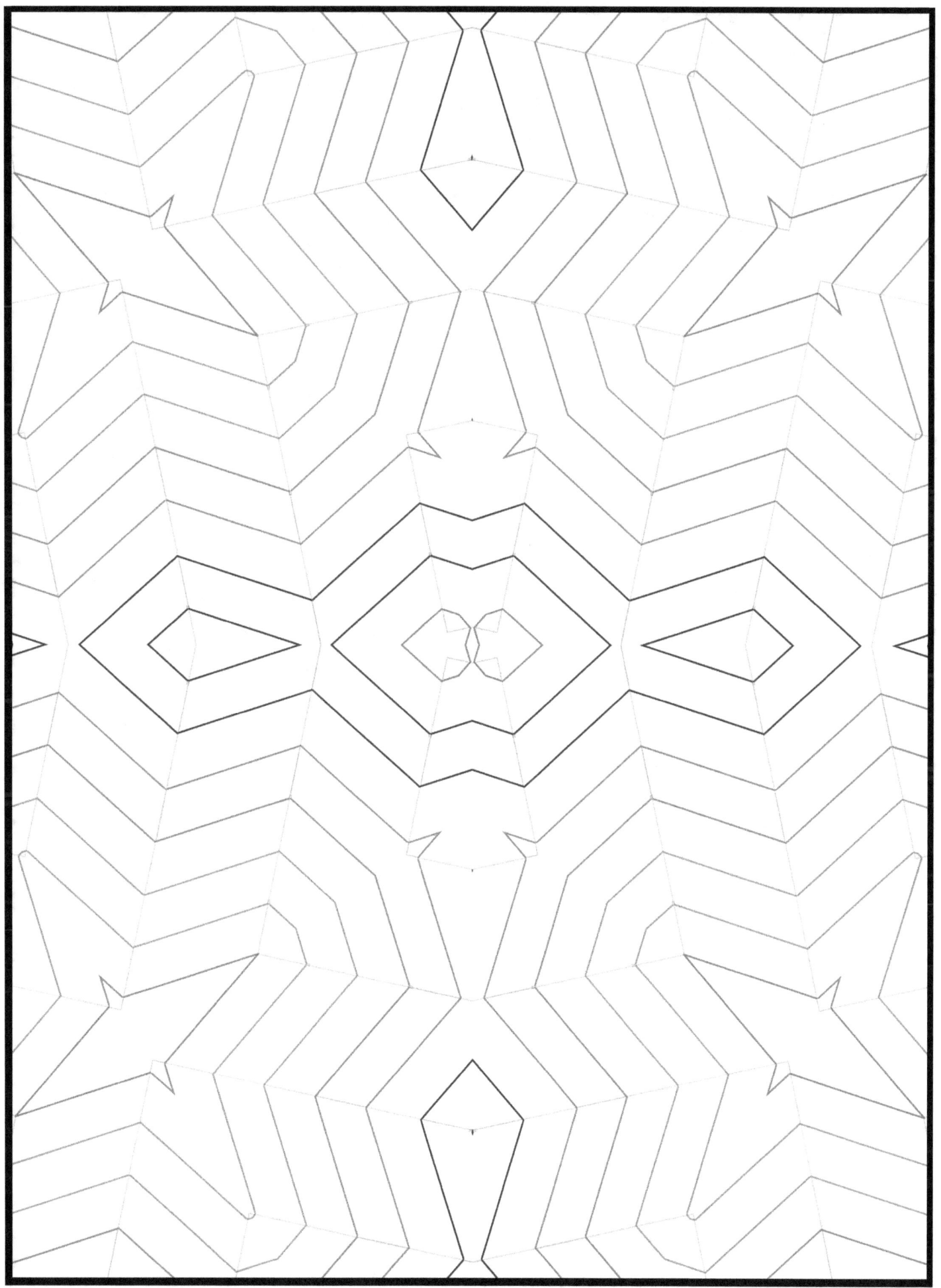

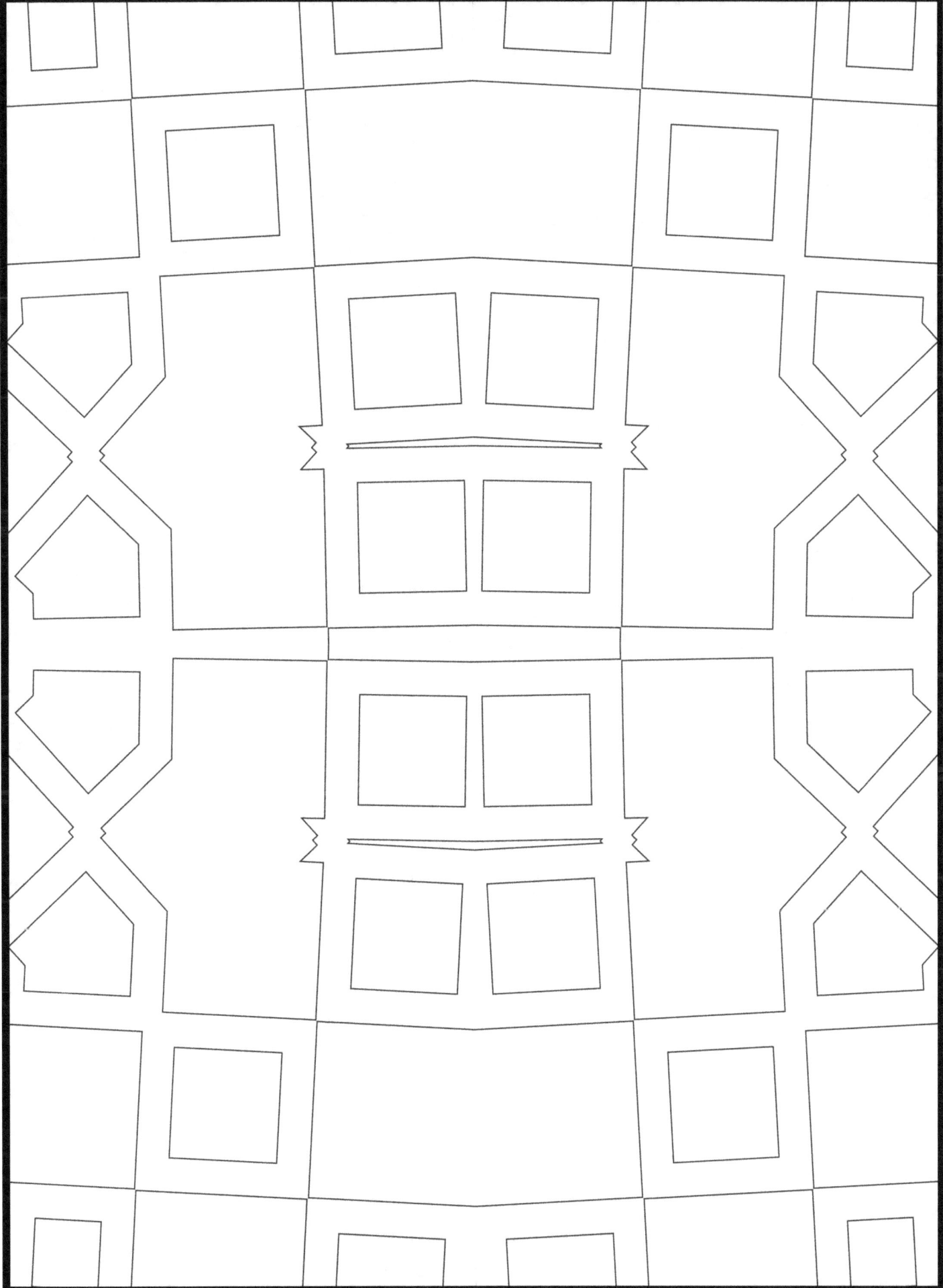

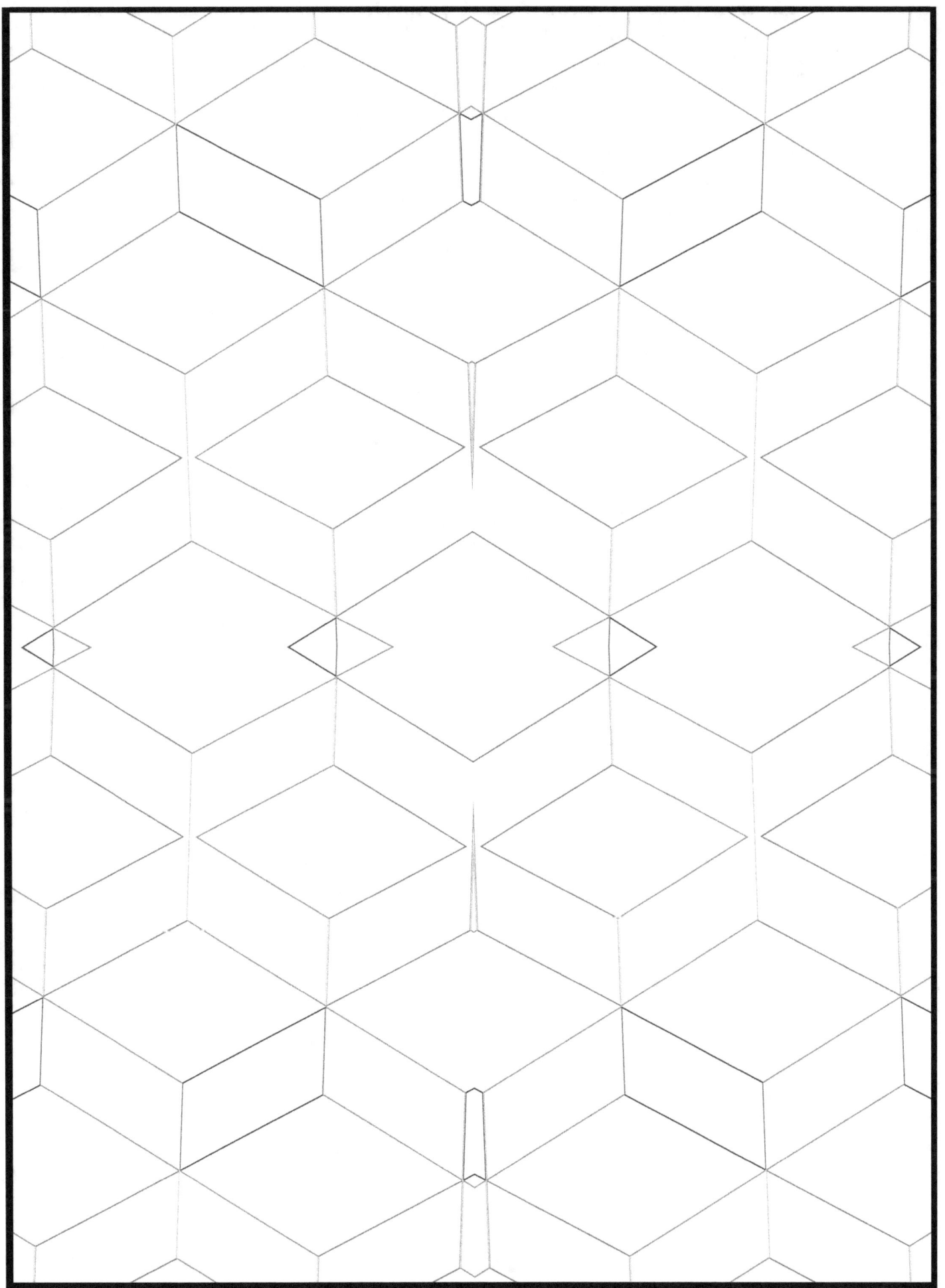

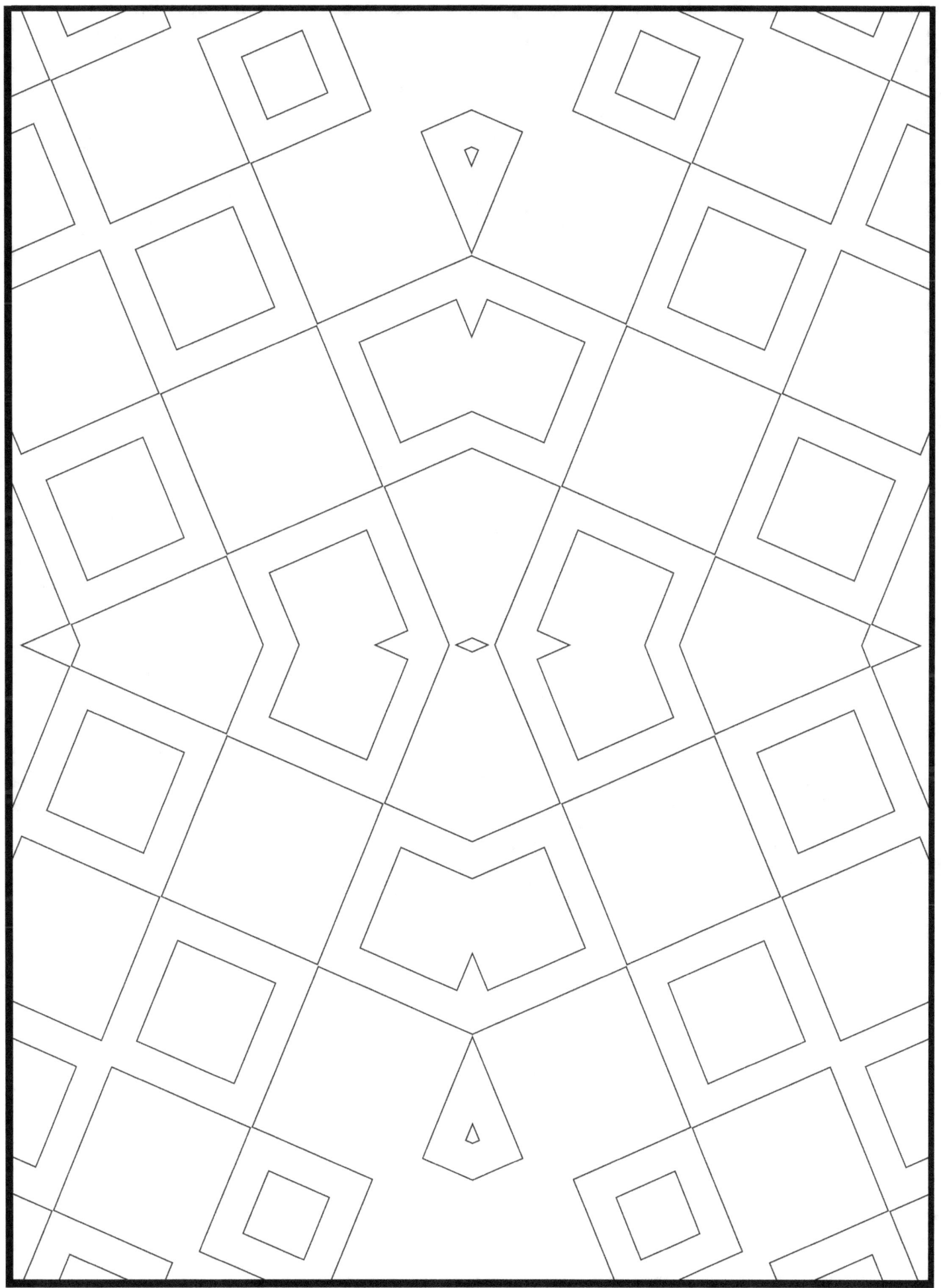

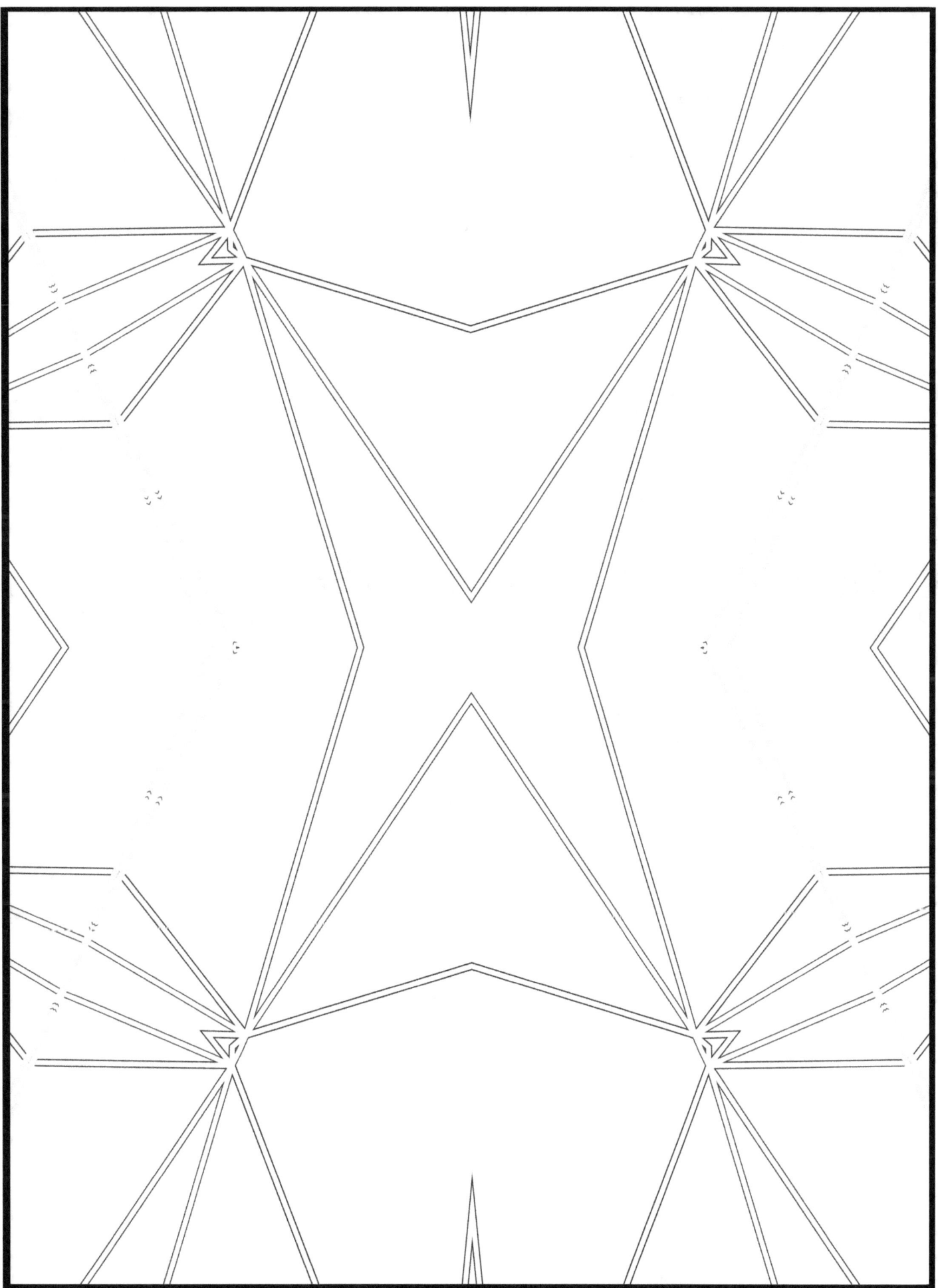

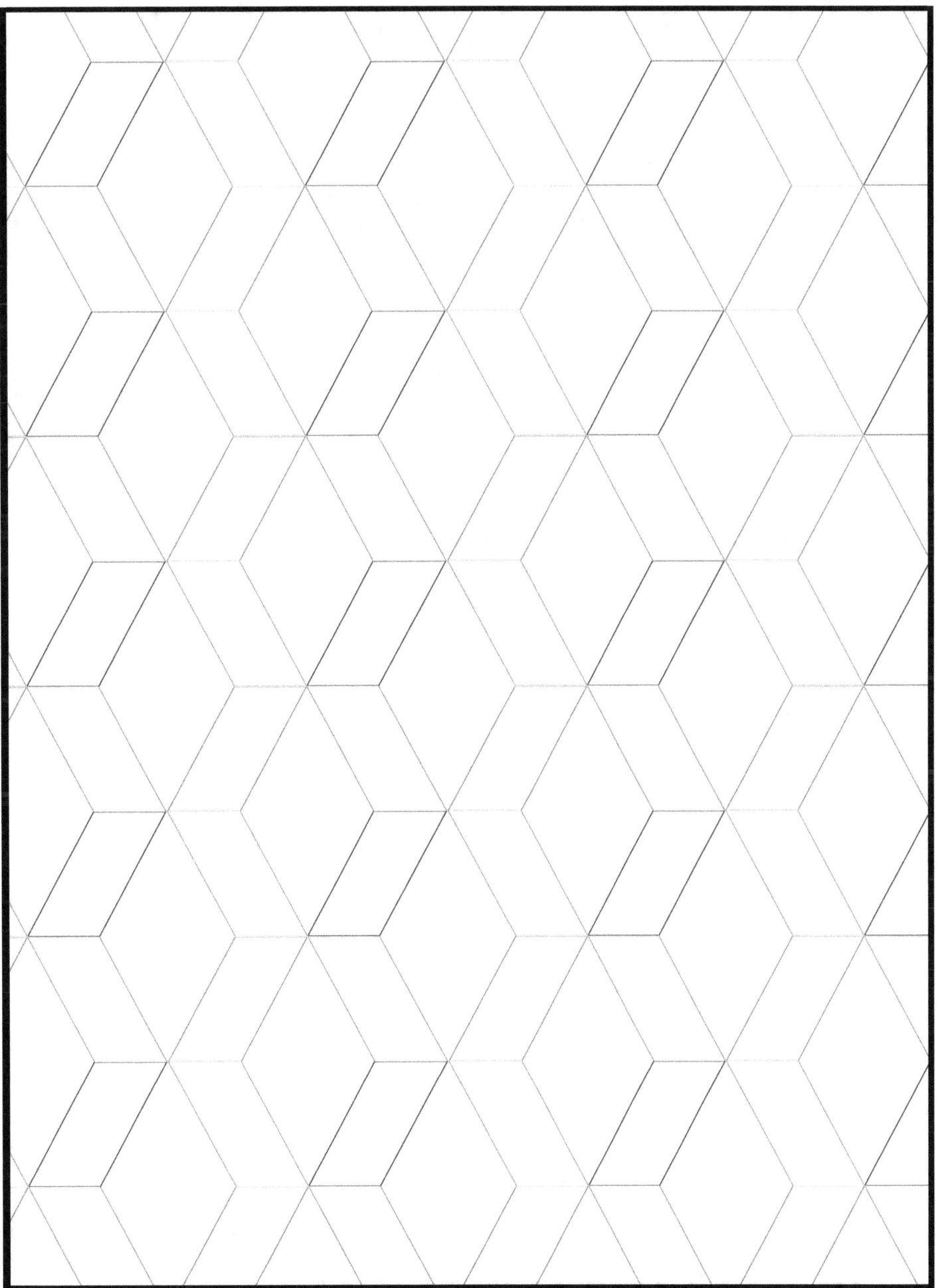

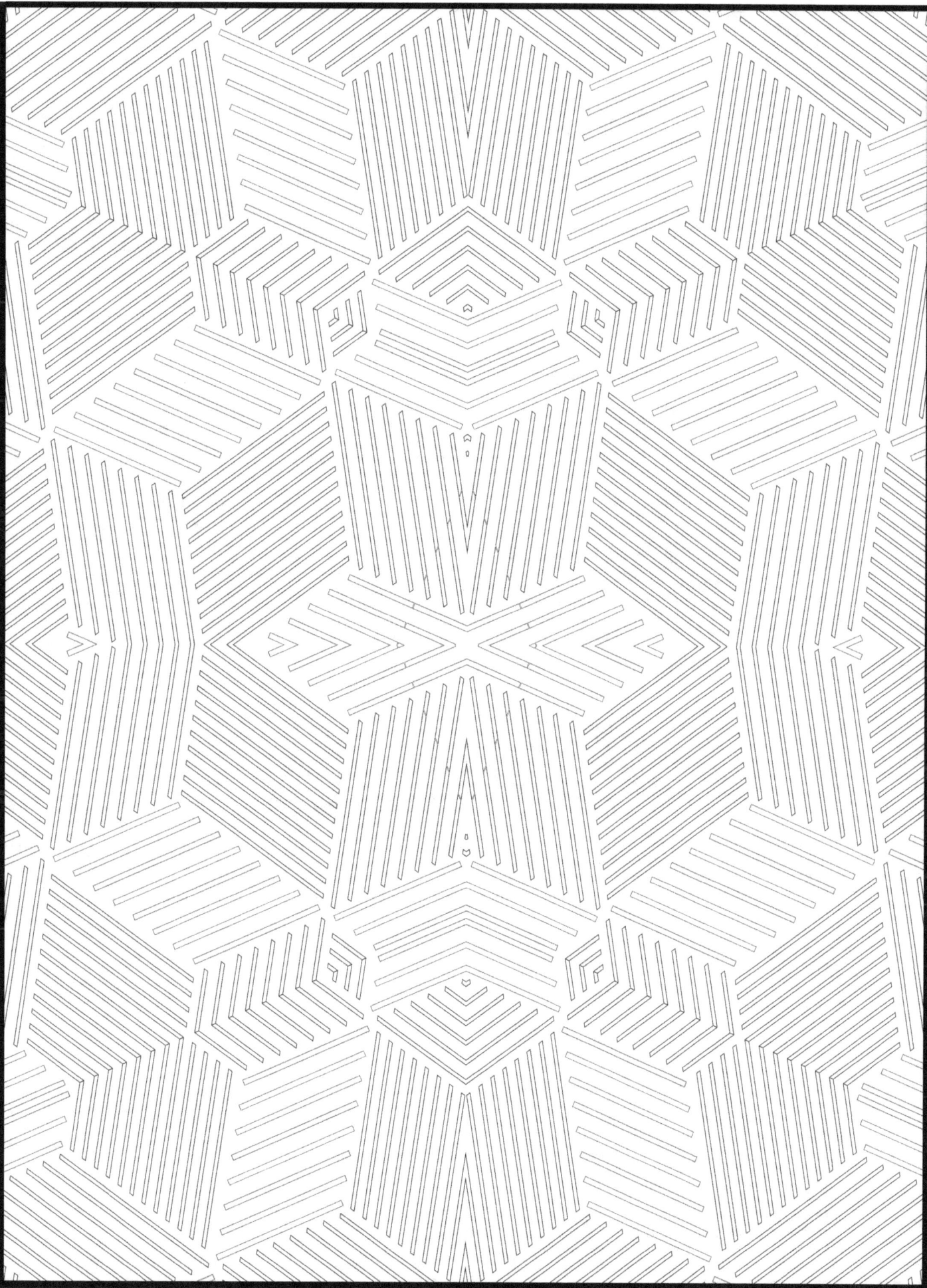

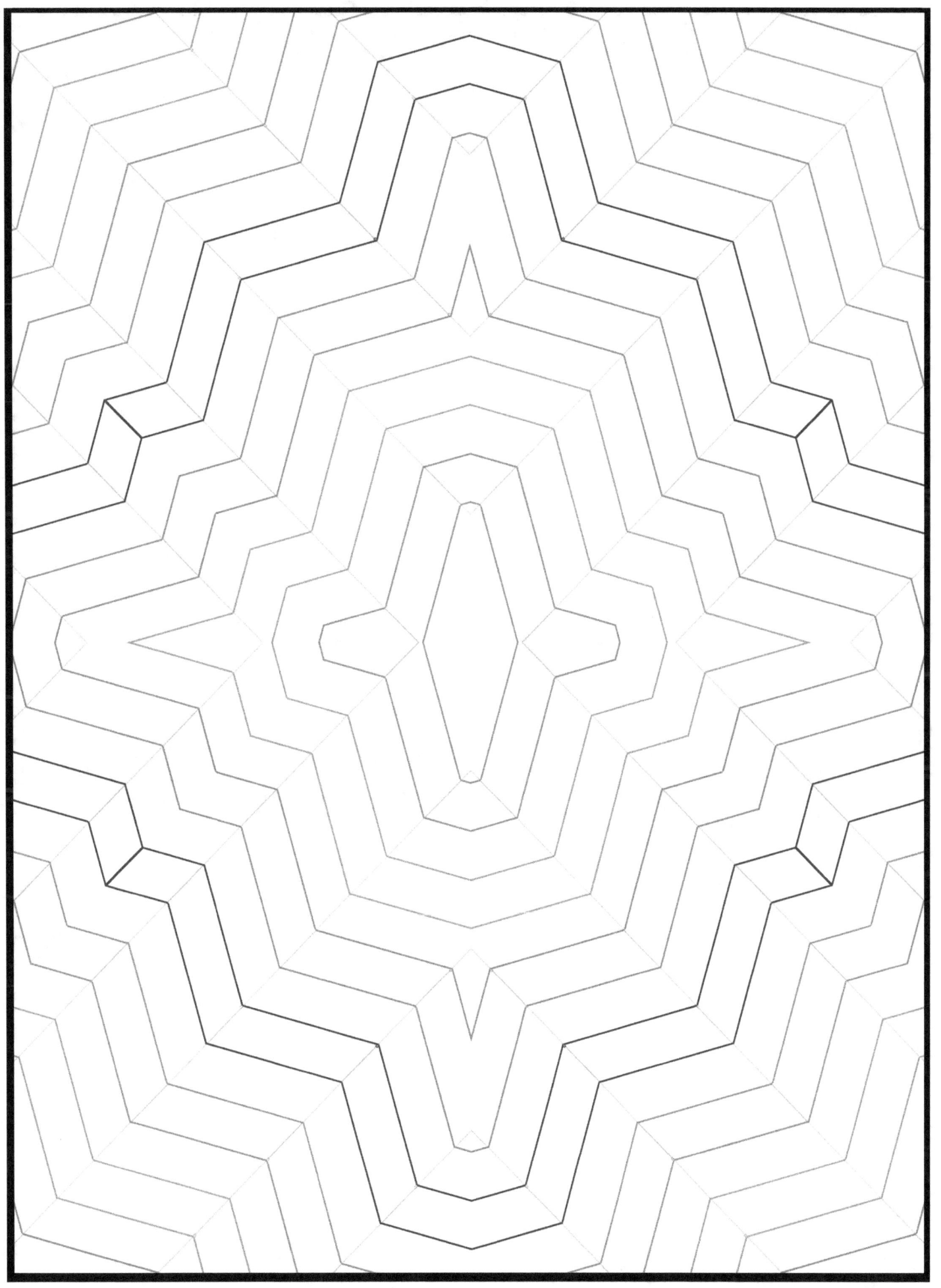

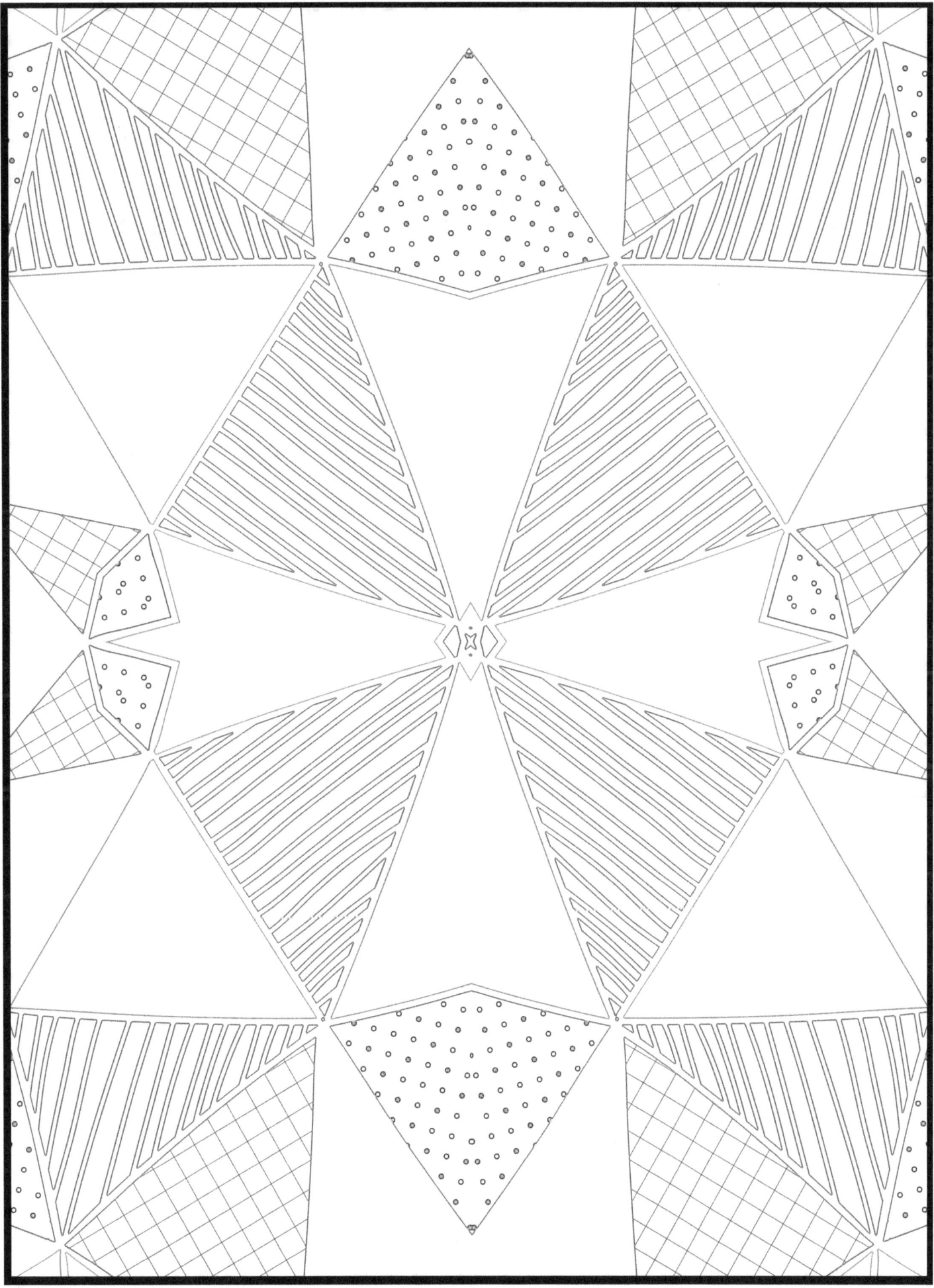

Thank you

Hope you've enjoyed your coloring experience.
We here at **VICTORIA** will always strive to deliver
to you the highest quality coloring books.
So I'd like to thank you for supporting us.

Before you go, would you mind leaving us a review on Amazon?
It will mean a lot to us and support us creating
high quality guides for you in the future.

To get notificate for next new Coloring Books
Please follow our Amazon Author Page.

Warmly yours,
VICTORIA Team